Original title:
Through the Roof of Time

Copyright © 2025 Creative Arts Management OÜ
All rights reserved.

Author: Helena Marchant
ISBN HARDBACK: 978-1-80587-173-6
ISBN PAPERBACK: 978-1-80587-643-4

## Celestial Reflections

Stars giggle in the night sky,
As planets trip over their own toes.
Asteroids dance quite awkwardly,
While comets laugh at their own woes.

The moon wears a silly hat,
Winking at the sun's bright beams.
Galaxies spin like a laughing cat,
Whispering cosmic, silly dreams.

**Journeying into the Infinite**

Time is just a winding road,
With squirrels hopping, unaware.
Each tick tock is a funny ode,
As clocks spin like they just don't care.

I packed my socks for space's trip,
But forgot my sandwich, oh dear!
What's a laugh without a blip,
In a universe full of cheer?

## The Architecture of Ages

A pyramid made of marshmallows,
Fell over with a giggle and bounce.
Ancient stones had funny fellows,
Building laughs that never trounce.

Columns made of candy canes,
In temples where the giggles grow.
History hides its silly pains,
Amongst the jokes that we don't know.

## Ascending Timeless Peaks

Mountains wear their hats of snow,
As peaks vie for the funniest hat.
Climbing up with a little tow,
Just to tease a passing cat.

The summit throws a silly party,
With laughter echoing all around.
Each cloud gives a joke so hearty,
In the heights where joy abounds.

## Whispers of an Ageless Dawn

In a land where socks lose their pairs,
Chickens debate the latest news flares.
Old clocks tick-tock, in reverse they spin,
While daisies dance, laughing, with a grin.

The sun wears shades, a cool, flashy style,
As it whispers secrets, all the while.
Cats in top hats drink tea with the moon,
Sipping on dreams that taste like balloon.

## Ascending the Spiral of Ages

A hamster spins tales on a wheel of fate,
While grandmas play bingo with a twist of fate.
Jellybeans burst with laughter and cheeps,
As rabbits read books that put mortals to sleeps.

Time unfurls like a spaghetti feast,
Noodles of moments, never the least.
Say cheese to the sun, it grins with delight,
And cupcakes start dancing, oh, what a sight!

### Chasing the Celestial Clock

I chased a shiny clock with legs adorned,
It giggled and taunted, my patience was scorned.
The stars sang old songs, a jazzy delight,
While comets played tag, oh, what a night!

Time flies like a bird in polka-dot shoes,
Sipping on coffee with colors and hues.
Worms in bow ties discuss quantum art,
While frogs leap through puddles, a merry old cart.

## Layers of Temporal Light

In a realm where cupcakes plot and conspire,
Chronicles unfold in a dance of desire.
The sun juggles planets, a cosmic charade,
While marigolds giggle in the shade.

Butterflies debate if they should wear hats,
And old trees gossip as wise, fragile chats.
Time wraps around, like a cat in a box,
Silly as it sounds, full of playful paradox.

## Symphonic Chimes of Lost Lives

In the attic where dust bunnies dance,
Old clocks giggle, giving time a chance.
They tickle the years with a cheeky grin,
While socks argue on what could have been.

A funny thing happened, oh what a sight,
A cat in a hat claims it's day, but it's night.
Pushing past hours with whimsical glee,
Time's just a joke, can't you plainly see?

The pendulum swings with a humorous quirk,
Lost moments conspire like they're all at work.
Chasing their tails, they trip and they fall,
Socks and socks argue, they don't care at all.

Each tick is a laugh, each tock is a tease,
Witty old timers just do as they please.
So let's raise a toast to the slips of the mind,
For every lost hour, joy is what we find.

## The Quest for Omniscient Stars

In pajamas, we plot our cosmos-bound flight,
Chasing stars, giggling into the night.
While aliens chuckle, they hide from our gaze,
Sipping space soup in cosmic cafés.

With telescopes made from old cereal boxes,
We decipher the skies, unsure if we're foxes.
Each twinkling wink is a cosmic prank,
Shooting stars giggle, they're never quite frank.

We map constellations with sticky-note flair,
Drawing blue whales and pokey hair bears.
Comets are sneaky, they zigzag through space,
Leaving behind breadcrumbs, they quicken their pace.

When dawn tips her hat, it's time for retreat,
But we leave with a joke, a soft little tweet.
The universe chuckles, its jokes hard to find,
Yet laughter's the treasure we seek in the mind.

## Echoes of the Unseen Dawn

The rooster forgot to wake the sun,
He snoozed away, oh what fun!
Chickens chuckled at the delay,
While coffee brewed, come what may.

Time slipped by in a tuxedo suit,
Dancing squirrels, oh what a hoot!
They juggled acorns, made a fuss,
Chasing shadows on the bus.

Old clocks grinned with hands that twirled,
Tickling seconds as they whirled,
Laughing at minutes in a race,
Taking ages to find their place.

So let's toast to time, my friend,
With laughter that will never end!
For moments wrapped in quirky glee,
Make every tick a jubilee!

## Whispers Beyond the Hourglass

Sandcastles built with grains of time,
Each grain a story, pure and prime.
The hourglass giggles with its load,
As time slips by on a squeaky road.

Tick-tock tickled the ancient trees,
They burst with laughter, if you please.
Branches swayed in a rhythm divine,
While squirrels swirled on the feline line.

The past wears socks that mismatch too,
A time traveler, just passing through!
With a wink, it dances in the breeze,
Forgetting years with utmost ease.

So let's whisper secrets to the air,
The future's waiting, unaware.
Turn the hourglass upside down,
And laugh as time forever spins around!

## **Fragments of Forgotten Years**

Old photographs stuck in a shoe,
Remind us that time flew right on cue.
Rats in the attic chuckle at fate,
While clocks are stuck, it's getting late!

We wear socks with patterns of cheer,
While memories drink from cups of beer.
Each laugh line etched in our skin,
Like an extra wrinkle where stories begin.

Time once tried to play hide and seek,
But it tripped and fell, oh so bleak!
Now it dances in the moonlit haze,
As we try to remember those quirky days.

So gather 'round, let's share our tales,
Of quirky hairstyles and odd scales.
For fragments of years, though they may roam,
Bring laughter to make our hearts feel home!

## **Celestial Shadows at Midnight**

The stars forgot their twinkle early,
They giggled in a cosmic hurly-burly.
Moonlight splashed like splattered paint,
Creating laughter that can't be faint.

Comets dressed in tails of flair,
Braided together, their cosmic hair.
They laughed as they zipped around the night,
Spreading giggles in their flight.

The planets spun like disco balls,
Ignoring the time when starlight falls.
Each constellation a jester's grin,
Tickling travelers who spin and spin.

So here we laugh beneath starlit dreams,
Where time is woven with silly schemes.
Celestial shadows break the silence,
Bringing forth laughter as a form of guidance!

## Winding Roads of the Ancients' Footsteps

Old paths of laughter twist and weave,
Where sunburnt stones play tricks up their sleeve.
Cartwheels roll in circles, oh what a sight,
Chasing shadows in the soft fading light.

Ancient trees dance with ghosts of old,
Whispering secrets that never get told.
Time takes a break, just for a while,
Making room for history's mischievous smile.

**Reveries Frozen in a Timeless Frame.**

Pictures hang crooked, still in their spot,
Grinning like jesters, they like it a lot.
A clock ticks backward, sipping some tea,
Counting the moments like it's a spree.

Shadows do jiggles while sunlight does wink,
Silly reflections in the bathroom sink.
Dreams wear pajamas, napping with glee,
While time does the limbo, carefree and free.

## **Echoes of Eternity**

Whispers of ages bounce off the walls,
Like echoes of laughter in endless halls.
Time plays the clown, wearing big floppy shoes,
Making everyone giggle, we can't refuse.

Tick-tock, tick-tock, the pendulum sways,
Telling tall tales of silly old days.
Faded echoes dance, twirling in fun,
Chasing the moonbeams until they all run.

**Celestial Vistas Above**

Stars in pajamas, giggling at night,
Dancing on clouds, oh what a delight!
Planets roll over, sharing a joke,
While comets are busy, puffing out smoke.

The moon wears a grin, just like a sly cat,
Winking at earthlings, "Imagine that!"
Galaxies giggle, twirling in space,
As time plays hopscotch in this cosmic race.

## Constellations of Old Memories

In the attic, dust bunnies play,
Chasing each other, come what may.
Socks from the past giggle and cheer,
Old shoes complain, 'Why are we here?'

Fridges hum tunes from years gone by,
While rubber bands plot to fly high.
Cereal boxes argue about crunch,
Old toys gather round for a lunch.

## The Silent Language of Forgotten Echoes

Whispers in corners, secrets so sly,
Papers crinkle as they pass by.
The clock ticks louder when tales unfold,
Of socks lost and stories retold.

In the kitchen, pots start to sing,
While spatulas flap like a bird on a wing.
Cookies rehearse for a taste test tonight,
Mysteries rise, oh what a delight!

## Starlit Pathways Through Memory's Veil

Under the bed where laughter hides,
Old baseball cards travel like tides.
Paper airplanes soar with a laugh,
While crayons debate who drew the best graph.

The sunbeams tickle the dust in the air,
As chairs gossip in a huddle and stare.
Banana peels roll with a flair,
Chasing their dreams without a care.

**The Dance of Shadows and Light**


In the moonlight, shadows swap shoes,
And giggle at the night's silly blues.
The lamp hums softly with tales of delight,
As cobwebs twirl in the soft, quiet night.

Dancing dust motes have all lost track,
Of where they've been, and can't find back.
They leap and spin with a bounce in their style,
Reminiscing of journeys with each little smile.

## The Pulse of Infinite Tomorrows

Looking ahead, where time does dance,
Chasing dreams with a silly prance.
Yesterday's coffee turns cold and sad,
But tomorrow's brew will make me glad.

Tick-tock goes the clock's funny beat,
Wearing mismatched socks on my feet.
Future adventures await with glee,
But first, I'll nap—just one... or three!

## Flickering Lanterns in Time's Labyrinth

In the maze of time, I lost my way,
Chasing shadows that laugh and play.
With lanterns flickering, they lead me on,
To ancient wisdom or maybe just brawn.

I stumbled upon a ghost with a wink,
Who offered me donuts, what do you think?
In the labyrinth, laughter echoes clear,
Yet I still can't find my left shoe, oh dear!

**Echoes of the Eternal Now**

Now is fuzzy, a wobbly thing,
Like a dog on a skateboard trying to spring.
Time is a joker, with tricks up its sleeve,
Juggling moments, making me believe.

Here's to the echoes of laughs once heard,
Like my cat that thinks it's a flying bird.
Whispers of chaos, and giggles galore,
In this timeless circus, I could not ask for more!

## The Canvas of Seconds and Seasons

Painting my moments in colors bright,
With seconds as brushes, such a funny sight.
A springtime sneeze, a summer sunburn,
Each stroke a memory that makes my heart churn.

As autumn leaves twist in a dance,
I trip over winter, given the chance.
In the gallery of life, I giggle and sigh,
For every fresh canvas, I say 'oh my!'

**The Cradle of Elapsed Moments**

Bouncing seconds like a ball,
Each tick giggles, oh so small!
Time's a jester at the fair,
Playing tricks without a care.

Moments tumble, slip and slide,
Like a clown on a wild ride!
Past regrets, a pie in face,
Oh what fun in a crazy race!

Countdowns dance in silly shoes,
Rolling time like it's good news.
Yesterday's a funny prank,
While tomorrow's on a plank!

In this cradle, we all sway,
Laughing at the games we play.
Elapsed moments, oh so light,
Ready for another night!

## A Canvas of Celestial Stories

Stars paint tales on midnight skies,
Each twinkle holds a sweet surprise.
Galactic giggles echo wide,
As comets dance with carefree pride.

Planets swap the latest scoop,
While meteors dive in a playful loop.
Alien artists throw some shade,
Crafting legends, unafraid!

In this vibrant cosmic haze,
Time becomes a wavy maze.
Sketches of the days long gone,
Where every laugh goes on and on!

Constellations, silly crew,
Chasing dreams where wishes grew.
On this canvas, bright and bold,
Celestial stories, laughter told!

**Dreams Shimmering in the Void**

In the void, where silence hums,
Dreams are like those ticklish drums.
Floating whims, a silly sight,
Chasing giggles through the night!

Whispers soar on cosmic wings,
Silly thoughts and funny things.
Wishes tumble, roll, and sway,
Drawing smiles to light the way!

Laughter twinkles in the dark,
Like fireflies with a little spark.
In this void, all worries cease,
Just joyful dreams that never leave!

Shimmering in what's unseen,
Where laughter reigns, a playful queen.
Join the dance, the timeless ride,
For silly dreams will never hide!

## Time Capsules of Spectral Light

Light beams bottle up the jest,
Capturing joy, a happy fest.
Timelines curled in puzzled shapes,
Tickling fate, oh what escapes!

Colors frolic in a jar,
As echoes bounce from near to far.
Past and future, laughing loud,
Sardonic grins from every cloud!

Every capsule holds a grin,
As moments join to spin and spin.
Wrapped in laughter's warm embrace,
Time's a prankster, full of grace!

In this glow, we twinkle bright,
Creating mischief with delight.
Spectral wonders, oh, what fun,
Time capsules burst—become the sun!

## The Alchemy of Memory and Time

In the cauldron of thought, I stir my age,
Crumbling past like cheese on a page.
With giggles and grins, my mishaps reside,
A potion of laughter, my trusty guide.

Time's a jester, it dances about,
With mismatched socks, it twists with a shout.
Years melt like ice cream, in summer's embrace,
In this carnival circus, I quicken my pace.

Memories bubble like soda in flight,
Pop! There goes last week's awful delight.
Yet here in the mess, there's joy in the trawl,
For every lost moment, I cherish it all.

A kite caught in wind, it swings with a twist,
Why did I wear sandals? Oh, what a list!
Yet laughter's a friend, in the folly of time,
Each giggle a spark, in this life's silly rhyme.

## Seasons in an Endless Loop

Spring rolls in on a skateboard wheel,
With flowers so bright, they dance and squeal.
Summer's a sunburn, a beach ball fling,
Where ice cream drips down, but who cares? We sing!

Autumn's a magician, with leaves in the air,
Sweaters pulled tight, oh, do I dare?
Winter's a prankster, with snow in my nose,
I slip and I slide, but in laughter, it goes.

The calendar spins like a top on its head,
Each month a reminder of joys we've shed.
Yet round and around, like a merry-go-round,
In the fun of the seasons, true bliss can be found.

So here's to the cycles, the whirl and the zip,
With each silly moment, let life take a dip.
We'll dance with the months, as they pass with a puff,
In this loop of delight, there's never enough!

## The Dome of Distant Lights

Beneath the bright dome, the stars start to wink,
Planets do pirouettes, as I spill my drink.
Galaxies giggle, like children at play,
Shooting stars tumble, and glide far away.

In this cosmic theater, I laugh and I stare,
Do those comets really care about my hair?
Each twinkle a chuckle, a wink from the night,
As aliens chuckle, saying, "What a sight!"

Gravity's a trickster, it pulls me along,
While I trip over stardust, humming a song.
The moon's just a dude, with a grin on his face,
And drops of pure starlight float freely in space.

Amid constellations, we dance on a beam,
A circus of wonders, a far-fetched dream.
In the dome of lost memories, we drift out of sight,
Where laughter is endless, 'neath stars shining bright.

## Waves Crashing on Timeless Shores

At the edge of the sea, waves tickle my toes,
With foam like whipped cream, the ocean just glows.
Seagulls are rascals, they stole my last fry,
Yet here on the shore, I can't help but sigh.

Tides flip like pancakes, they rise and they fall,
The sand's like a blanket, inviting us all.
With buckets and shovels, we build castles tall,
Only to find them washed away with a call.

Each splash is a giggle, a swish and a swirl,
I toss my hat up, watch it flip and twirl.
The sun is a buddy, with rays that take flight,
As I splash in the water, everything feels right.

On shores without time, where laughter won't cease,
The waves sing a tune of whimsical peace.
So here's to the ocean, its joke-telling ways,
In this splashy adventure, I could spend all my days!

## Fractals of Light and Time

In a world where clocks tick backwards,
Laughter lingers in the air,
A cat wearing glasses reads the news,
While unicorns steal my favorite chair.

Jellybeans dance on sunny rays,
Whispers bounce off candy walls,
Each tickle of time brings silly plays,
As squirrels race down candy halls.

The moon wears socks, so bright and neat,
Jesters juggle with bouncing stars,
In this fractal fun, life is sweet,
We toast with fruit punch in giant jars.

So let's flip the hourglass upside down,
And spin in circles till we fall,
In this comical, timeless town,
We find our joy in the silliest hall.

## **The Pulse of the Unseen Clock**


A clock with no hands spins like mad,
Its tick is a giggle, loud and clear,
Time wears a tutu, quite the fad,
While gnomes ride bicycles, full of cheer.

The seconds skip and jump about,
Singing songs of pancakes and pies,
In a realm where time's a playful scout,
And the sun wears clogs as it slowly flies.

You'd think it's chaos, but it's divine,
With cookies falling from the sky,
As we dance and sip on sparkling wine,
Underneath the rainbow, oh my!

So let's toss seriousness away,
And embrace the silly that makes us glow,
In the pulse of laughter, we sway,
Time's a comedy show, don't you know?

## Skylights of Forgotten Joys

Above the clouds, a party brews,
With rainbows made of jelly beans,
The stars wear shades, they dance and choose,
To twirl around like silly scenes.

A forgotten joy pops like a spark,
As balloons float high on lemonade streams,
Where whispers of laughter fill the park,
And time checks in, just for dreams.

Clouds wear pajamas, cozy and bright,
As sunshine plays hide and seek,
Every moment spins in pure delight,
While lightning bugs dance, so unique.

So let's find those skylights, break the mold,
Where joy is found in the simplest ways,
In this dreamy escape, colorful and bold,
Together we'll dance through the whimsical maze.

## **Weaving Threads of Time**

In a loom where minutes twist and twine,
We craft our jokes with colorful threads,
Time gets tangled, it's really quite fine,
As kittens knit cozy hats for beds.

Weaving laughter in each little stitch,
As gnomes bring cupcakes, frosting ablaze,
And in each loop, we find a niche,
Where happiness grows in quirky ways.

The fabric of moments, soft and bright,
Is wrapped around all our fun desires,
Where unicorns play chess in twilight,
And laughter ignites like brightening fires.

So let's play tag with the sands of time,
And wear our joy like a funny crown,
In this tapestry, so sweet and prime,
We'll dance through days, never feeling down.

## Moments Pitched in Eternity

A sock went missing, that old thief,
It sparkled once, now brings me grief.
Time plays tricks, I laugh and pout,
Chasing dust bunnies, that's what it's about.

The cat leaps high to catch a dream,
While I just sit and plot and scheme.
A calendar's full but all we find,
Are doodles and jokes left behind.

Yesterday's lunch is now a quest,
With crumbs of laughter, we digress.
Time's a jester, settings shift,
Each tick a giggle, each hour a gift.

So here we dance, on life's tightrope,
Balancing slips with tools of hope.
In moments pitched, we take our flight,
With chuckles riding on the night.

## **Flavors of Lost Memories**

Candy wrappers from age-old treats,
Whisper tales of sugary feats.
Flavors blend in a wobbly swirl,
Time's a chef with a goofy twirl.

Soda fountain, where laughter flows,
Mixing smiles with fizzy prose.
A mustache made of whipped cream,
In a world where silliness gleams.

The taste of laughter, a savory blend,
With each giggle, sweet joys transcend.
Forgotten spices, a dash or two,
In recipes meant for me and you.

So let's nibble on joy, let's feast on cheer,
In this banquet of time, hold dear.
With flavors alive, we'll pretend and sway,
As we savor the moments that giggle away.

## Bridges Over Temporal Rivers

We cross the stream with a funny boat,
Rickety planks and a rubbery moat.
Each step a story, a comedic slip,
As wiggly fish join us on this trip.

With gears and springs, clocks play along,
Tick-tock rhythms become our song.
Jumping between ages, a silly dance,
Laughing at fates as time takes a chance.

Riddles from the past come out to play,
In the game of life, we find our way.
Cracking jokes 'neath a cosmic beam,
Through waves of laughter, we surf and dream.

So gather 'round, let stories unfold,
On bridges that shimmer with timeliness bold.
With every share, let giggles ignite,
As we wander through moments so bright.

**Dimensions Beyond the Now**

Welcome to a world of wibbly-wobbly,
Where time is silly and quite fobbly.
Dimensions dance on a bounce and giggle,
In the cosmic playground, we twist and wriggle.

Doors that lead to jellybean skies,
Balloons that talk, oh how they surprise!
The past is a puppet, the future a clown,
Together they juggle, never let down.

Interstellar laughter bounces in phase,
Shattering moments in technicolor haze.
We leap in the rhythm of whimsical flight,
In this endless sketchbook of day and night.

So grab your hat as we take a spin,
In dimensions where giggles begin.
Let's float on the whims of time's playful song,
With hearts wide open, we cheer, we belong.

## **Driftwood of Days Past**

Float me back on lazy tides,
Waves of laughter, twisting rides.
Memories lost like socks at sea,
Nestled in the sand with glee.

Coconuts that tell tall tales,
Pirate ships and windless sails.
With each splash, a slip and slide,
Time's a prankster, can't divide.

Gnome and goblin share a drink,
Beneath the stars, we laugh and wink.
Catfish dancing, quite absurd,
Who knew thoughts could be so blurred?

Bottles tossed, secret notes,
Dancing in our leaky boats.
Floating past that grinning moon,
Days like these end far too soon.

## Luminescent Horizons

Bright horizons tickle souls,
Sunsets blend with candy rolls.
Butterflies and taco trucks,
Spinning tales of witchy ducks.

Glowing signs that wink and play,
Calling dreamers in dismay.
Stars above, a silly sight,
Twinkling, chuckling through the night.

Dandelions, giggling high,
Blow a wish, let giggles fly.
Jumping puddles, splashing fun,
Time takes flight, we dash and run.

Radiant dusk, a funky vibe,
Each tick-tock, a joyful jibe.
We wave goodbye as shadows dance,
In the glow, we take our chance.

## The Fabric of Fluctuating Hours

Stitching moments into dreams,
Past the seams, reality beams.
Pockets full of silly laughs,
Time's a jester, weaving crafts.

Whirling clocks with floppy hands,
Jumping beans in time's commands.
A tapestry of whoopee pies,
Fleeting glances, absurd highs.

Unraveled threads of bright delight,
Sparkling seams with every night.
Tangled up in laughter's reel,
Life's a dance, oh what a deal!

Mismatched socks and clashing hues,
Strolls along the path of blues.
Each hour wrapped in giggles tight,
In this fabric, we take flight.

**Skylines of Yesterday's Dreams**

Skyscrapers made of cotton candy,
Chasing rainbows, feeling dandy.
Clouds of popcorn float above,
Loving life, what more to prove?

Zebra planes on paths of cheer,
Sing of flights we hold so dear.
Yesterday's dreams in silly hats,
Riding high with goofy cats.

Sunbeams twirl in vibrant spree,
Dancing shadows, wild and free.
Montaged laughter fills the skies,
As the day again complies.

Jellybean stars spark the night,
Frolicking in a sweet delight.
Life's a canvas, paints a gleam,
In these skylines, kiss a dream.

## Mosaics of Yesterday's Dreams

In the attic, dust bunnies dance,
Prancing like youth in a funny trance.
Old toys giggle, and shadows sneak,
Waving goodbye to the past they speak.

A clock with no hands just tells jokes,
Tick-tock, it giggles at silly folks.
Pictures that wink from their gilded frames,
Remind us life's but a game of names.

Paper airplanes fly with flair,
While socks on the ceiling claim the air.
Each laugh echoes stories of days gone by,
As memories chuckle and gently sigh.

## Frequencies of Forgotten Monuments

In the park, statues talk, it's true,
A pigeon's coo is their DJ's cue.
They throw a party for all to hear,
While squirrels DJ with nuts and cheer.

Grass blades hum along with the breeze,
A symphony played by the buzzing bees.
Echoes of laughter from kids on a swing,
Monuments shake as they start to sing.

Old benches share tales of lovers sweet,
With floppy hats and mismatched feet.
Together they laugh at their marble plight,
As the sun sets, painting things bright.

## The Orchestra of Endless Moments

Conductors wave their silly batons,
As raindrops tap like playful pawns.
Balloons float up in a merry swarm,
Creating a symphony rather warm.

Clocks with violins play off-beat tunes,
While shadows dance like children on dunes.
A harmony of giggles fills the air,
As light-hearted memories linger there.

The stage is set with fickle fate,
While rubber ducks contemplate their state.
In the spotlight of an afternoon glow,
Time smiles as the world steals the show.

## Tapestry of Fleeting Whispers

Woven threads of cheeky delight,
Spin tales of bamboo, stars, and flight.
Ghosts of whispers share jokes so sly,
In the fabric of dusk, they marvel and fly.

A tapestry of giggles fills the space,
Where snickering dreams find their grace.
Socks and slippers have stories to tell,
Of grand adventures in the laundry's swell.

Each stitch holds secrets of laughter unspun,
In the world's quilt of joy, everyone's won.
As night drapes softly and moonbeams gleam,
A chorus of whispers chases a dream.

## Tales from the Edges of Infinity

Once I met a clock that ticked,
It laughed so hard, the hands just kicked.
We danced around a loop so tight,
Then tripped and fell into the night.

A rabbit jumped right through my dreams,
With pockets full of silly schemes.
He pulled out snacks and shouted, "Whoa!"
I snacked on time – what a show!

The stars all giggled in a flash,
"Hey, look at us!" they made a splash.
I said, "You're late, but that's just fine!"
They winked and chewed on space and time.

So here's a tale of moments tossed,
Where laughter lives and time gets lost.
The edges stretch and bend around,
In this odd place, joy is found.

## Conversations with the Ghosts of Time

I spoke with ghosts on a comfy chair,
They sipped on tea without a care.
"Your hair looks great, did you just style?"
They floated 'round and laughed a while.

One claimed to know the future's game,
Pulled out a crystal, wasn't the same.
I asked about my next big date,
"Just try not to trip, you'll be just great!"

They told me stories of days gone by,
With jellybeans, they'd make me cry.
A ghost slipped on a rubber duck,
And suddenly it just ran amok!

In whispers soft, they shared their tales,
Of grand adventures and silly fails.
For every moment they had cried,
They found a laugh they couldn't hide.

## The Boundless Horizon of Moments

I stood on edges of time and space,
With goofy seconds—what a race!
They threw confetti, oh what fun!
And then they giggled, "We've just begun!"

Each minute wore a silly hat,
Jumping and jiving like a cat.
"Toss me a sandwich while you're at it,"
I caught the bread, oh please don't sit it!

The laughter blew like bubbles in air,
Floating away without a care.
A moment winked, tipped its bright shoe,
And whispered, "Come dance, it's all about you!"

So here's to days that stretch and leap,
With wobbly hours that do not sleep.
Let moments tease and time unwind,
In this grand tapestry, fun we'll find!

## Lighthouses in the Sea of Time

Deep in the sea where time just winks,
Lighthouses giggle, or so it thinks.
They blink and flicker like fireflies,
Guiding lost ships with silly sighs.

One lighthouse sang a tune so loud,
It chased away the gloomy cloud.
Its beam of light was made from cheese,
And made the waves just dance with ease.

A ship sailed by, all sails askew,
With crew who painted everything blue.
"Is that a lighthouse or a fish?"
They bumped and laughed, fulfilled their wish.

In ripples of time, their joy won't stop,
As moments giggle and brightly hop.
While lighthouses shine in colors bright,
They keep our laughter alive at night.

## Eclipses of Forgotten Epochs

When the past forgets the present's name,
Time trips over its own silly game.
Old clocks laugh as they tick-tock slow,
Hours have parties, but no one will know.

Yesterday's socks still dance in the air,
Waving goodbyes without a care.
The sun took a nap but the moon kept the beat,
While minutes played tag on the old cobbled street.

In the attic of moments, dust bunnies reign,
Joking with time like it's all just a game.
Calendars dangle like piñatas on strings,
Waiting for laughter, for joy that it brings.

Time trips on its laces, falls into the past,
Chasing its tail, what a sight unsurpassed!
Nostalgia in bloom like a quirky old vine,
Whispering secrets of when years were a line.

## Gazing Beyond Yesterday's Eaves

Peeking through windows of yesterday's glee,
I spot a cat chasing a time-travel spree.
Calendars juggling in funny old hats,
Mice in boots dancing with quirky old rats.

Future and past play hopscotch on the floor,
With giggles echoing from the open door.
Time's up on the wall with its hands in the air,
Scolding the seconds, 'Not so fast, beware!'

A slinky of seconds coils up and unwinds,
Each loop a memory left far behind.
Past and present share tea with a dame,
Both raise their cups for a time-twisted game.

Yet I laugh at the paradox weaving its spell,
Days like confetti in a whimsical well.
Stars gossip loudly like they're in a race,
Winking at time with a cheeky old face.

## The Prism of Passing Moments

Rainbows slip through the cracks of the day,
Moments collide in a colorful fray.
Time does the cha-cha, with glances and spins,
The past wears pajamas, let the giggling begin.

A kaleidoscope of seconds shines bright,
Dancing reflections in jubilant light.
Yesterday's jester juggles the sun,
While shadows join in, just having their fun.

An hourglass tumbles down to the floor,
But beads of the past just laugh and implore.
Moments like bubbles float high in the air,
Popping with giggles, without a care.

As time bends backward with a comical grace,
I chase after laughter, a nonsensical race.
Each tick of the clock is a grin in disguise,
Where every second is a silly surprise.

## Reaching Beyond the Temporal Sea

Waves of moments crash in a playful spree,
Surfing on laughter, making time feel free.
Seashells whisper tales of sand in the breeze,
As hours get tangled in giggling trees.

Each tide carries echoes from long ago shores,
Where time wears a swimsuit, strikes funny poses.
Droplets of memories roll off like confetti,
Splashing in puddles, isn't life petty?

Bubbles of laughter float, drift, and sway,
Time's just a kid wishing for another play day.
With seas full of shenanigans waiting to bloom,
Every tick is a party; it goes 'boom boom!'

Gazing at the past with a comical smile,
As time does the merengue, just for a while.
Reaching for moments where the sun always beams,
In a sea of old giggles, life dances in dreams.

## Where Past and Future Intertwine

I met my past on a Monday,
Wearing socks of purple and gray.
It asked if I had found my way,
I chuckled, 'Not today!'

A glimpse of future in a hat,
Claimed it knew a secret mat.
I said, 'You can't be serious,
With shoes that look so various!'

So we danced in circles strange,
While laughing at our tangled change.
Time winked like a crazy clock,
As seconds turned to laughter's flock.

In this circus of the hours,
We twirled and spun like lilac flowers.
A comedy of clocks and bells,
Where all was fun, and time just swells.

## A Symphony of Fleeting Glimpses

In the orchestra of bygone days,
A trumpet toots in silly ways.
The past takes lead, in polka dots,
While futures dance in dapper knots.

A fiddle plays a funny tune,
As memories flit like a balloon.
In this festive grand parade,
We giggle, while we serenade.

The harmony of laughs and grins,
Like cats in hats, where humor spins.
Each note a wink, each chord a cheer,
As moments jiggle, bright and clear.

So join the chorus, clap and cheer,
For time's a jester, full of cheer.
With strings that stretch from here to there,
We laugh aloud, without a care.

## The Mirage of Hours Elapsed

In a desert of forgotten dreams,
The clocks melt like ice cream streams.
I chased a minute, slipped it fast,
It giggled, 'Time's a trickster blast!'

A mirage danced, with flip-flops bright,
While whispering tales of day and night.
I thought I'd catch a fleeting second,
But it dashed away, just like a beckon.

The sands of time, they swirl and twirl,
Like whirlwind skirts in a pretty whirl.
Each grain a jest, a playful nod,
Reminding me I'm just a clod.

So I jive with shadows of the past,
And laugh at futures rushing fast.
In this mirage, I lose my way,
But oh, what fun to sway and play!

## Secrets Written in the Grain of Sand

On shores where whispers softly land,
I found old secrets in the sand.
Each grain a giggle, each beach a jest,
I wondered if time really gets some rest.

As waves rolled in with a splashing cheer,
They tickled toes, whispered, 'We're here!'
The past shouted 'Hey!' while the future blushed,
While moments embraced, in laughter, they rushed.

I built a castle that tipped and swayed,
Each tower a story, freshly made.
Then nature winked, and down it crashed,
'It's just time,' I sighed, 'Our fun's not dashed!'

So here I stand, with grains in hand,
Collecting secrets from this merry band.
With laughter echoing through the strand,
Time's a prankster, oh so grand!

## Beyond the Veil of Time

A clock that tocks with feet of clay,
Skipped past the noon in a funny way.
The past is a draft that needs more spice,
Worms in the apple, rolling the dice.

With socks on hands and hats askew,
We learn to dance in a world askew.
Riding the breeze on a paper plane,
Chasing the antics of silly rain.

Tickling seconds, we jump and twirl,
Time's a balloon that begins to swirl.
Our laughter echoes through dreamlike halls,
Like ticklish ghosts at the end of calls.

Hats off to time that makes us grin,
With a wink, it lets the fun begin.
In this laugh-trap, the seconds sing,
Who knew time had such a funny wing?

## Steps on the Stairs of Infinity

Climbing up steps that wiggle and bend,
Each one we hop seems to have a friend.
Stairs that giggle and play hide and seek,
A trip on the way makes our knees go weak.

At the top, there's a flip-flop parade,
Where clocks dance silly and dreams are made.
Bananas in hats take the lead on squid,
While jellybeans lead a conga, no bid.

"We're lost!" we cry, but the sky just winks,
Throwing us blueprints and pink polka dots.
With wishes and giggles, we float like a boat,
Across rivers of candy and soda-soaked floats.

So let's give those steps a joyous cheer,
For infinite giggles are really here.
Each leap, a tickle, a light in the air,
We slide down on rainbows—oh, what a dare!

## **Traces of Timeless Journeys**

In a land where gnomes play hide and seek,
With shades of mischief on every peak.
A squirrel in goggles shoots past with flair,
"Watch out!" it squeaks, with an acorn to spare.

We ride on the whims of a ticklish breeze,
Through forests of candy and chocolate trees.
Each step that we take leaves a sprinkle behind,
Like breadcrumbs of giggles, one of a kind.

The trails cross paths with a sneaky cat,
Who's plotting a nap on a silly hat.
In the echoes of laughter, we chase the light,
While shadows perform a hilarious fight.

So join in the dance of these timeless twirls,
Where dreams like confetti spin, dance, and twirl.
Through traces of fables and stories sublime,
We tangle our feet in the fabric of time.

## Spectrums of Lost Moments

A rainbow of laughter spills down from the sky,
Where yesterday's socks wave a jolly hi.
Moments like bubbles pop out with a splash,
Tickling our feet in a wild, goofy dash.

Neon thoughts tumble like colors in flight,
Chasing the shadows, they dance with delight.
While time does a jig to an off-beat song,
We stretch out our arms, where the absurd belongs.

Snapshots of chaos, caught in a spritz,
Like pies in the face from those cheeky little wits.
"Who threw that?" we giggle, then point to the sun,
Because nothing says laughter like silly ol' fun.

So gather those moments, your spunky confetti,
In the spectrum of time, let's keep things ready.
For every lost tick is a chance to invoke,
The dance of the ticks that are ever bespoke.

## The Tides of Temporal Dreams

In a world where clocks just tick,
Fish wear hats, they're quite a trick.
Time slips glibly like a bar of soap,
And all our plans dissolve like hope.

Beach balls bounce in backward flight,
While seagulls squawk, they're quite a sight.
A jellyfish, with shades of blue,
Sings serenades, with a wink, just for you.

Sandcastles crumble at noon's embrace,
Yet somehow, they still win the race.
Life's a game of hopscotch round,
Where laughter echoes and joy is found.

As waves get tangled in a knot,
We dance along, forgetting what's hot.
With every tick, the fun's the prize,
In this silly world where time just flies!

# Remnants of Stars in Dust

Once I caught a star with a net,
Said it dreamt of jellybeans, you bet!
We shared a laugh in the cosmic brew,
While planets giggled, all bright and blue.

Cosmic dust fell like sugar rain,
Into my tea, it caused disdain.
Yet sipping starlight was a joy,
Who knew galaxies had such ploy?

Time's an owl wearing spectacles,
Giving wise advice but so flexible.
"Don't take a second too seriously," it said,
As asteroids danced, twirling instead.

Galactic giggles filled the skies,
As planets don their shiny ties.
With shooting stars playing peek-a-boo,
Remnants of laughter are born anew!

## Shattered Moments in Stillness

Moments fall like pancakes, hot,
But leave a syrupy mess, I thought.
Time's a jester, playing pranks,
With silly hats and funny thanks.

Seconds blink like fireflies bright,
While whispers of echoes laugh at night.
Cups of joy spill at the seams,
Shattered fragments of scattered dreams.

Tick-tock, the old clock gasps,
As misshapen shadows curve in laps.
What once was solemn, slips and falls,
Into a pool of giggles and brawls.

Stills become a water slide,
And I just laugh; I cannot hide.
Each fragment shines, a glittering vast,
In this world where smiles come first and last!

## Chronos Dances on Starlit Shores

Chronos waltzes in flip-flop shoes,
His dance ignites the cosmic blues.
With moonbeams lighting up his way,
He jigs with time, come join the play!

Galaxies spin like tops so fine,
While constellations sip on wine.
Time's a game of musical chairs,
With stars in hats and no one cares.

Tickled by the cosmic breeze,
Chronos spins with utmost tease.
As grains of sand become confetti,
Come do the dance, hope you're ready!

With laughter echoing soft and bright,
We raise a glass to the starlit night.
While time, it twirls with graceful odds,
On the shores where laughter nods!

## Vistas Beyond the Matrix of Time

In a world where clocks giggle and chime,
I trip over hours like they're silly slime.
Butterflies dance on seconds all day,
Oh, to catch the moment is child's play!

Past and future swirl in a waltz,
A laugh as my memories skip and vault.
I chase the minutes, they tease and dodge,
Dancing on whims, like silly mirage!

In a meadow where yesterday's jokes reside,
I roll on the grass with time as my guide.
Each tick-tock a punchline, funny and bright,
Joking with hours that float like a kite!

So let's laugh with the hours, make merry, oh dear!
For time is a prankster, let's give it a cheer!
With each fleeting moment, let's gad and weep,
In the garden of giggles, we'll happily leap!

## **Horizons of Liminal Spaces**

In the spaces where whispers collide,
Gigglers and dancers all share a ride.
Between here and there, there's room for a jest,
Where time does the limbo, giving its best!

I peek through the gaps and see folks flail,
Gravity's lost, and so is the scale.
Floating on wishes, we bound through the air,
While minutes keep tumbling without a care!

Like doughnuts in orbit, we spin, spin, spin,
Our laughter the fuel, let the ride begin!
Slipping and sliding in temporal streams,
Chasing the echoes of absurd dreams!

So join this bizarre, liminal dance,
Where time is a joke in a comic romance.
With every weird second, we twirl and we play,
In spaces of laughter, come join the fray!

## Nightfall of Ancient Echoes

As shadows grow long in the zany dusk,
I hear echoes of laughter, where absurdities rust.
The old jokes awaken, like ghosts in a hive,
Whispering punchlines—a giggly jive!

So here's to the ancients, timeless and spry,
Tossing their quips like confetti in sky.
Their whispers tickle the night like sweet dreams,
Time's not a straight line; it's curvy with beams!

They're crafting their mayhem with giggles so bright,
Painting the stars with jokes made of light.
"Once upon a tick," one ancient declared,
"The funniest moments are really well shared!"

With nightfall around, let's dance with the past,
Those echoes of humor forever will last.
Time giggles and wriggles—a riotous space,
Where laughter's the treasure time can't replace!

## Celestial Corners of the Past

In corners celestial, where stardust does play,
I gather old giggles, like stars in bouquet.
Launching nostalgia like rockets in flight,
In the comical cosmos, I wiggle with light!

A nebula of chuckles, swirling around,
Time hiccups and wobbles, joyfully unbound.
Each twinkle a chuckle, each star a delight,
Can cosmic humor outshine the night?

I laugh with the comets that zoom on their spree,
Telling tales of the past, cosmic glee!
They loop through the ages with humor and grace,
In the theater of time, it's a comic embrace!

So let's sail through these corners, held tight in a grin,
For laughter is timeless, and where we begin.
Each moment a jewel in this cosmic jest,
In celestial corners, we giggle and rest!

## Time's Veil: A Hidden Passage

Underneath layers, we sneak and slide,
The clocks are laughing, there's nowhere to hide.
Just a tickle in space where we spill and giggle,
Past and future shake hands, doing a little wiggle.

The cat with nine lives has booked a late flight,
While socks lose their partners, quite the silly sight.
We dance with our shadows as days zip by,
Saying 'hello' to the past, as the moments fly.

Nostalgia's a prankster, sharp as a whip,
Stealing the candy while we take a sip.
Winding our watches with jelly and cream,
Feeling the mischief of time's endless dream.

With snapshots of laughter stored in a box,
Who knew the past was filled with silly pox?
We hop on a comet, let's ride and play,
Skipping through moments that giggle away.

## The Breath of Yesterday's Wishes

Wishes past bubble like soda in glass,
Tickling our noses as we giggle and pass.
We chase the dreams from yesteryears' seams,
Prancing like kids on birthday cake beams.

A turtle sails backward, it's quite a sight,
Sipping on laughter under soft starlight.
The smiles of yesterday ride on our socks,
Tying our memories in crazy, fun knots.

Lollipops shimmer with secrets untold,
While the winds whisper tales both funny and bold.
We wear time like a hat, skewed and askew,
With glittering echoes of everything new.

Silly sunbeams tumble, spin and collide,
Waving at shadows that dance in our stride.
The breath of the past gives us all a tickle,
As we savor the sweet of the moments that spickle.

## Reflections in the River of Ages

In waters where giggles ripple and splash,
Reflections wiggle like coins in a stash.
We dive in with chuckles, rafts made of dreams,
Navigating currents of whimsical streams.

Old jokes float by, wearing hats full of dust,
Ticklish ripples, in laughter we trust.
With each splashy memory, we spin with delight,
Building bridges of funny to dance through the night.

Fragments of time wear the silliest shoes,
Concocting a cocktail of wild, vibrant hues.
The river swirls backward, quite the funny plight,
Splashing through giggles, we bubble with light.

As ducks quack in chorus, they gossip and tease,
Sharing the secrets that float in the breeze.
Reflections in giggles, my heart feels so free,
Time is a jester, just smiling with me.

## When Echoes Turn to Whispers

Echoes bounce back with a mischievous grin,
Tickling the air as they twist and spin.
Whispers of laughter drift soft on the breeze,
Silly yet tender, like teasing soft cheese.

They say time has layers, like a good pastry,
Baking up memories, nothing too hasty.
Slicing them thin, we savor each bite,
Finding the sweetness that hides in the light.

The clocks do a jig, under shadows they waltz,
While moments of humor pop like small faults.
When echoes grow quiet, and whispers take flight,
We dance in the silence, all giggles and light.

The laughter of ages just tickles our ears,
As stories unfold over giggly beers.
So here's to the echoes, both silly and spry,
For in laughter, we find how we endlessly fly.

## The Lantern of Lost Days

In the attic, dust bunnies dance,
While yesterday's socks take a chance.
A lantern flickers, giving a wink,
As shadows play and the clocks rethink.

Time's a jester, with tricks up its sleeve,
It steals your youth, then asks you to grieve.
Yet here we are, with giggles and grins,
Chasing the past, oh where to begin?

Old photos chuckle, their colors are bright,
While musty tales weave through day and night.
Oh, what a ride on this carousel flip,
We laugh at the time, take another sip!

So raise a glass to those hours that flew,
Each moment's a gift wrapped just for you.
With lanterns aglow, let's jive through the days,
And chase our old selves in humorous ways.

## Metronome of Eons

Tick-tock, the metronome swings,
Counting our blunders, and all silly things.
With every beat, we tumble and twirl,
Time laughs at us; oh what a whirl!

A rhythm of woes, a tempo of cheer,
We dance awkwardly, yet hold it dear.
As time skips along, we flail like a fish,
Wishing for moments that taste like a dish!

Oh, the ancients would chuckle at our pitter-patter,
They'd roll their eyes at our mindless chatter.
But we march to our own offbeat refrain,
In this grand symphony, we're all insane!

Every second's a twist, a tasty surprise,
With laughter and hiccups, we rise with the highs.
So may this metronome tick ever on,
As we juggle our days like a clown on the lawn!

## Pilgrims Across Eternal Skies

Look! Pilgrims prance on clouds of marshmallow,
With backpacks of giggles, they've got quite the show.
They float on dreams, sipping stardust tea,
Not a care in the world, just pure jubilee!

Beneath them, earthworms are snapping their toes,
While daisies in tutus join in with the prose.
Stars wink in delight, the moon rolls its eyes,
As pilgrims defy logic in whimsical skies.

Each soars on a whim, a comet of laughs,
Trading tales of blunders and silly mishaps.
Who needs a map when you have a bright grin?
With laughter leading, it's easy to win!

So here's to those travelers, endlessly bold,
Who swirl through the cosmos like stories retold.
May we join in their frolic, and scatter our sighs,
As pilgrims forever, in our own funny skies!

## Resounding Windows of Life

Open the windows, let laughter creep in,
As life throws its punches with clumsy spins.
Each day's a vivid, uproarious twist,
With moments so quirky, they simply persist.

Windows rattle as giggles ensue,
While walking the line between silly and true.
The echoes of joy ring louder than pain,
As we paint our days in humor's bright stain.

Peeking outside, those clouds start to giggle,
The sun snaps a joke, as the raindrops all wiggle.
With every new breeze, a chuckle floats by,
A reminder to smile, let your spirit fly!

So let's raise our voices, in unison sing,
To the resounding windows that life loves to bring.
With laughter and warmth, may our hearts ever shine,
Through the windows of life, let's dance and align!

## Fragments of Forever

A clock struck twelve, then one, then more,
I lost my socks, who knows where they floor?
The minutes tickle, they play hide and seek,
While I just dance in my fuzzy old peak.

Yesterday's hair was a wild, green spree,
My glasses fogged up, can't quite see the tree.
I found time wrapped in a sandwich of cheese,
And waited for laughter to float in the breeze.

Each second's a joke, a fantastical ride,
As I trip over dreams I've long tried to hide.
The years pass by like a circus parade,
With elephants juggling life's grand charade.

So here I stand, with a grin like a kid,
In the gallery of moments, where time often hid.
Let's raise a toast to the fragments we chase,
In the whimsical dance of this beautiful space.

## Time's Infinite Canvas

The brushes of seconds paint colors anew,
With splashes of laughter in brilliant hue.
I spilled my tea, watched it swirl and swirl,
As the canvas of life gave a playful twirl.

A portrait of chaos, it tickles my mind,
With pictures of past that are comically blind.
A self-portrait made out of mismatched socks,
While time winks at me from its quirky clocks.

The past is a canvas, a riotous spree,
Where moments are sketched in wild jubilee.
As I step back, I can't help but decree,
That blending the years is the best kind of key.

With laughter as paint, I'll create my own shade,
In this whimsical world where time never fades.
So here I stay, with my brush held up high,
Painting life's moments while time giggles by.

## Beyond the Crumbling Hourglass

The sand squeaks softly like shoes in the hall,
As I race against time to catch my own fall.
With gravity's giggle and time's silly play,
I stumble on dreams in a most comical way.

The hourglass grumbles, its shape starts to twist,
"Who needs a schedule?" it whispers in mist.
I watch as the grains make an impromptu dance,
While I try to keep up, but I lose my own pants.

A tumble, a fumble, a wonderful mess,
Catching memories like butterflies in a dress.
Each second's a jester with tricks up its sleeve,
In the circus of time, it's all make-believe.

So I chuckle and chase as the moments take flight,
In the absurdity found in the depth of the night.
With laughter and silliness lighting the way,
I find joy in the mess, come what may.

## Windows to Yesterday

I peek through the window and see my past dance,
With clowns and confetti, each silly romance.
A puppet in pajamas, a cake on the floor,
As laughter erupts from the front to the door.

In yesterday's garden, I trip over light,
With juggling dreams that take flight in the night.
The panes giggle softly, reflecting my grin,
As I step into memories wrapped up in a spin.

Time wears a hat that is far too tall,
With patches of moments that bumble and sprawl.
The whimsies of ages are peeking at me,
With winks and confetti, how funny to be!

So let's laugh at the past like a whimsical song,
As we dance through the windows, where we all belong.
With joy in our hearts and a skip in our feet,
The echoes of laughter are the sweetest retreat.

www.ingramcontent.com/pod-product-compliance
Lightning Source LLC
Chambersburg PA
CBHW070320120526
44590CB00017B/2755